GETPRESENT

{
Simple Strategies *to*
Get Out *of* Your Head *and*
Lead More Powerfully
}

SARAHARVEYYAO

ip

inlet
publishing

Erik —
am so happy to know
you and be
in your
presence!
Sara

Published 2013
Printed in the United States of America
ISBN: 978-0-9899509-0-9
Library of Congress Number: 2013954079

For information, address:
Inlet Publishing
20126 Ballinger Way NE #132
Seattle, WA 98155

(CONTENTS)

(INTRODUCTION)

*"The intuitive mind is a sacred gift and
the rational mind is a faithful servant.
We have created a society that honors
the servant and has forgotten the gift."*
—Albert Einstein

AS AN EXECUTIVE COACH for the past thirteen years, I have been deeply immersed in the development of leaders, and I have personally trained and coached more than 3,500 leaders around the world. Many people ask me how I can work with executives and not be intimidated, especially since I started in leadership development when I was merely 27. Seeing the humanity of a leader, no matter their cultural background, position, or level of power, comes easily to me.

My father was the president of a major public utility company, and growing up I was surrounded by executives. At the age of twelve, I was trained by Lou Tice, one of the "grandfathers" of the human potential industry. In high school, my father let me observe his leadership team meetings, and over dinner, we discussed what I sensed about people and what behaviors I witnessed. I attended Board of Director's dinners and witnessed how business was "really" done in the '80s. I was immersed in leadership at an early age and saw the good, the bad, and sometimes, the ugly.

After receiving my BA in Organizational Communication, I immediately got into corporate training, earned my Master's degree in Organizational Management, and landed a job doing what I loved most—developing leaders. I worked with a diverse group of leaders and started noticing distinct patterns among them. Most were prone to working crazy hours, stretching themselves thin, reacting emotionally, striving to prove their worth, and constantly thinking about either the past or the future. I didn't know it at the time, but the miles I put in driving and flying the world to work with leaders from various countries was the beginning of my life-long fascination and unofficial research of leaders, as well as the start of my own personal journey toward presence.

I left my corporate job in 2002, and since then have been working with thousands of clients via my own consulting practice (www.yaoconsulting .com). In 2007, after having two boys and growing my business, I, too, was feeling the effects of working at a fast pace, being stressed, and uninspired. As a result of my own unease, I was propelled into a period of profound personal growth. I studied for several years with a variety of people, including a spiritual teacher, a Jungian rolfer, and several mind/body awareness practitioners. I ventured on a personal journey into the practice of presence and it changed my life, my health, my relationship, and my work with clients. For me, I found the root cause of my own stress was my lack of presence in the moment. I was living from my head, cut off from the inner wisdom of my heart and gut. I committed to shifting the way I worked, and when I saw my own life experience shift in profound ways, I was naturally drawn to share these practices with my clients. Since 2010, I have focused my entire business on helping leaders develop their own presence. The results have been consistently compelling.

I wrote this book for leaders, both in the traditional sense of the word—meaning they are leaders in their companies or communities—but also for people who may not consider themselves a traditional leader. To me, a leader is anyone who has the opportunity to influence another person. This book is for those who are hungry to experiment with strengthening their ability to be more present—with their employees, families, friends, colleagues, and community members—

and who wish to experience the wisdom and joy available from being in the moment. In the chapters that follow, we will explore the definition of presence, as well as specific and actionable tools and techniques to help you get started with strengthening your own practice of presence.

CHAPTER 1:
(WHAT IS PRESENCE?)

"The most precious gift we can offer others is our presence. When mindfulness embraces those we love, they will bloom like flowers."

—Thich Nhat Hanh

PEOPLE OFTEN USE THE word presence to describe another person's impact, energy, and intensity: "He has a strong presence," or "I could feel her presence." In fact, this is why most companies hire me—to help leaders strengthen and improve their presence. Throughout this book, I will address how to strengthen the quality of presence. The first step is strengthening your ability to be present.

Being present is the ability to pay attention in the moment, on purpose. When you are present, you are able to tune in to a deep awareness of everything you are experiencing in any given moment. You are aware of your own experience-your body's responses, thoughts, and emotional reactions. When you are in the moment, you can also tune into other's experiences and reactions, gaining access to important data, both visible and not. When you are present, you are a non-attached observer of the moment.

HOW PRESENT ARE YOU?

Think back over your day today. How often do you think you were truly paying attention and being present? Take this quick quiz to help you determine how present you are during a typical day. Check the box if the accompanying description is something you experience on a regular basis.

❏ You have a hard time quieting your mind when you're going to sleep or you wake up during the night with your mind racing.

❏ When you reflect back on your drive to or from work, you can't remember the details.

❏ You don't notice when you're hungry and thus tend to skip meals/snacks.

❏ You forget conversations you had the hour, day, or week prior.

❏ You forget people's names shortly after you are introduced to them.

❏ You don't notice body aches or pains until they impact your activity level.

❏ You don't always hear what others are saying because your mind is elsewhere.

❏ You don't really notice the music on the radio while driving.

❏ You regularly leave things at home that you need for your day.

❏ You sometimes find yourself in a bad mood or irritated, but you don't know why.

❏ You have a hard time focusing on one thing at a time.

❏ You miss out on quality time with your loved ones, because you're thinking about something else.

❏ You use your laptop or other devices while attending meetings.

❏ You don't notice you need to use the restroom until it becomes urgent or painful.

❏ You sometimes lose track of how much you've eaten or how much you drank.

❏ When a loved one asks how your day was, you have a hard time remembering what the first half of your day was like.

If you checked 4 or less: Not bad! You likely go through your day staying fairly present. Your opportunity is to deepen your presence to your emotions and body sensations, tuning into the unspoken dynamics of a room.

If you checked 5-9: This is pretty common! I suspect you have plenty of moments feeling present and then experience an equal number of moments where you feel less conscious or as if you are "just going through the motions" of your day. Your opportunity is to strengthen your presence muscle, so you can gain access to even more information that you may have missed.

If you checked 10 or more: You are in for a treat! Your busy twenty-first century life may have gotten the best of you, and the good news is that if you're reading this, you have all sorts of opportunities to improve the quality of your work and life and feel much better through the practice of presence.

No matter how you scored, know that everyone has room to strengthen their ability to be present, and it's simply a practice. Consider it a muscle you build over time; one that you will have the opportunity to strengthen. Unless you're incredibly enlightened and have studied these concepts for a while, you will have room to deepen your practice and experience for even better results. Even for me, after experimenting with being present for years now, I notice how often I have opportunities to deepen my practice.

Most of us have had plenty of moments when we felt grounded, calm, and really solid. Can you think back to the last time you felt this way? That's what it feels like when you're present. Presence doesn't mean you're necessarily happy all the time, but someone who is present tends to feel a sense of peace, unattachment, and/or strength.

On the contrary, when we're not present in the moment, we can be scattered, easily agitated, and stuck spinning in our heads. When you're in this state, you are essentially operating from an unconscious state. Unconsciousness is like living and working from within a fog. We tend to not see things clearly, our senses are dulled, our minds spin, and we easily "forget" or never notice the subtleties of each moment.

Being present and fully aware in the moment is our *natural* state. We come into the world fully aware, curious, and connected. It's only through the conditioning of our mind that we stray from the purity of our presence. The practices in this book aren't about learning anything new; rather they are about remembering. My hope is to help you remember how to come back to your natural state of presence and to all of the richness and wisdom that comes as a result of being in our truest, most natural state.

WHY BEING PRESENT IS SO HARD

Being present is a simple concept, but it's not easy to do. Try this practice: Close your eyes, take a few deep breaths, and simply try to tune in to how your feet feel on the floor. Try and see how long you can hold your attention on only your feet. When you notice your mind start to wander or you have a thought, open your eyes. No judgment, just experiment with how long your attention can stay on your feet

My suspicion is that it didn't take long for your mind's chatter to kick in. If so, that's quite common. Our twenty-first century lives demand that we're constantly connected, work at a rapid pace, and juggle many different logistics. Our minds are constantly "on," thinking, strategizing, and worrying about the past or the future. The habit of "being in your head" so often makes it even harder to become present. Asking you to flex your atrophied "pay attention in the moment" muscle is a tall order.

The bombardment of information and electronics doesn't make being present any easier. We are constantly fed stimuli via the web, TV, email, and Facebook, not to mention countless other sources. *TIME Magazine* conducted a poll of 5,000 people, and 84 percent of respondents said they could not go one day without their cell phones. Fifty percent of the respondents said they sleep with their phones nearby, and 24 percent said they check their phone or email every 10 minutes.[1] It's possible for us to become addicted to the stimulation of the incoming information as if it's a drug. The varied and intermittent stimulus of checking email or the web gives us a hit of dopamine-one of the "feel good" chemicals in our brain. From our brain's perspective, that constant stimulus is not that different from being addicted to cocaine. We have trained our brains to constantly "get a hit." Attempting a shift to being present or paying attention on purpose is even more difficult, because we're swimming upstream from a cultural and brain-chemistry perspective.

When you think about strengthening your ability to be present, it's helpful to know the developmental trajectory you might experience. One of my favorite models for gaining mastery in something new is Maslow's Four Stages of Learning.

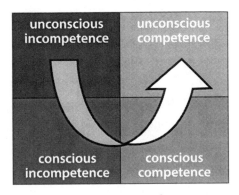

Maslow's Four Stages of Learning

When you look at the four quadrants you can see that you start with unconscious incompetence and make your way forward toward unconscious competence. The process is as follows:

1) **Unconscious Incompetence:** you don't know what you don't know.

2) **Conscious Incompetence:** you know what you don't know.

3) **Conscious Competence:** you have learned what you need to know, but you're ultra-conscious of your new behavior and need to "think" about how to do it.

4) **Unconscious Competence:** the new skill has become so engrained in your brain, you don't have to "think" about doing it; it comes naturally.

Understanding this model is helpful in a couple of ways when thinking about the skill of presence. As you're strengthening your ability to be present, you will work your way through each of these stages. You may not even know how often you behave unconsciously, but as you build your presence muscle, you'll become aware of how often you *aren't* paying attention. Then you'll start to pay attention more, but still need to think about doing it. Eventually the behavior will become second nature to you, and you will experience all the benefits without working at it.

The second reason understanding this model is important is because one of the hardest things to do is to become conscious of the things you are unconscious to. Repatterning your mind to become conscious—especially of actions you have competency in—is a journey. I encourage you to please approach it as such. The point is not to achieve perfection right away, if ever. The point is that you become a bit more conscious as frequently as you can. In the following chapters, I will take you through specific steps, exercises, and experiments to help you become more present, more often.

THE COSTS OF UNCONSCIOUSNESS

If you're not living in the present moment, you are living in a state of unconsciousness. Of course, there are different extremes of this, but the truth is, you're either present or you're not. When we live from an unconscious state, the side effects and the consequences can eventually become painful. Throughout my years of experimenting with presence and working with many leaders from varied industries, I have witnessed the painful results of not being present. The symptoms can manifest at an individual level or a collective one, which can include teams, organizations, or companies, and depending on the severity, the costs can be anywhere from inconvenient to downright devastating to an organization.

The Costs to the Individual

In 1997, I started a new job as Training Manager in a telecommunications company. I was also engaged and excitedly planning our wedding. One day during my lunch break, I dropped my car off to get an oil change and while waiting in the lobby I made several phone calls to keep the wedding planning moving forward. Feeling pleased with my efficiency, I quickly walked through the parking lot to grab a quick bite. My mind was on all the things I needed to do when I got back to the office. Suddenly, I felt a sharp pain in my right foot. I had rolled my foot into a pothole that I didn't notice. I hobbled my way to get lunch, practically hopped back to my car, and drove myself back to work. I felt determined not to be slowed down by my injury. It wasn't until an hour later when I was in unbearable pain that I asked a co-worker to take me to the hospital. I had broken my foot. My unconsciousness caused me physical pain, but guess what else it did? It slowed me down enough to get my attention. Eventually, when I was stuck on a couch for several weeks, I realized how very NOT present I had been.

Our lives have a way of doing this. When we consistently live from a place of unconsciousness or a lack of presence, it inevitably creates suffering. One of the fastest ways suffering gets our attention is through the manifestation of physical pain. When I broke my foot it caused me to "wake up" from the dominance my mind had over me, and it brought my attention to the present moment.

Have you experienced something similar? Or maybe you know someone who has experienced pain or suffering at a physical level? Perhaps their back went out, they broke a bone, or even had cancer or a heart attack, but as a result, they discovered the event brought about clarity and a deeper understanding of their life or purpose.

If consistent unconsciousness doesn't manifest itself in physical pain, it might manifest itself in emotional, mental, or even spiritual pain. The famous Swiss psychotherapist Carl Jung believes that depression, anxiety, and a sense of emptiness are all manifestations of living from a state of unconsciousness or lack of presence. From an adult development perspective, this lack of consciousness tends to come to a head around mid-life or middle age. According to Jung, our forties and fifties are the natural time in our development as adults when a deeper level of presence is ripe to emerge. These are the years when we naturally start thinking of our bigger purpose, legacy, and meaning. This development process is the origin of the "mid-life crisis," but how that unfolds for each individual is based on how present you are with what's trying to come forth.

When we pay attention to changes in our emotions, bodies, and minds, we don't have to experience a crisis at all. But for those not paying attention or in that unconscious state, their lack of presence can result in what you might think of as a typical mid-life crisis, such as a divorce, focus on materialism, or a mono-focused ambition. At any point we can alleviate the psychological pain by simply turning our attention to it. Become present or conscious of the pain instead of denying it. The bottom line is that pain in any form can be a doorway to a higher level of living, relating, and being. It's the ignoring, denial, or choice to remain unconscious that is the source of the true pain.

The Costs to the Collective

Living from a lack of presence costs us our health, puts stress on important relationships, slows career growth, and can stunt our spiritual development. When a collective group, such as a team or company operates from a lack of presence, it often manifests as a group or collective dysfunction. The symptoms of that dysfunction can vary from unproductive conflict management to a lack of efficiency or a stagnate bottom line due to a lack of innovation. Patrick Lencioni, author of *The Five Dysfunctions of a Team* outlines these dysfunctions as five major themes including: absence of trust, fear of conflict, lack of commitment, avoidance of accountability, and inattention to results. Any unproductive group behavior you see at work will fall into one of these five dysfunctions.

Here's an example of how a team's group unconsciousness resulted in dysfunctional behavior. As part of my consulting practice, I regularly observe leadership team meetings as a way to develop coaching objectives for my client. In 2008, the president of a mid-sized manufacturing company invited me to attend his leadership team meeting. During the meeting, my client asked his team about a number on the sales report. Specifically, he asked what the sales result would be if they made a different decision. Right after he asked for the new number, each of the eight meeting participants pulled out a calculator (including the president) and started "running the numbers." As an outside observer, I found this lack of efficiency and precision fascinating, but when I asked my client about it, he had no idea that each team member was using their energy this way—and it's no wonder since his head was buried in his own calculator!

No one in the room questioned or frankly was even aware of the lack of efficiency their team suffered from. Or if they did, they certainly didn't say anything. Just for fun, my client and I ran a calculation on the cost of the team operating from an unconscious place. We calculated only time and salary for one week, and we only calculated when the members of the leadership team were involved in unproductive meetings. The cost of one week of unconsciousness for this company was more than $75,000. Keep in mind, this calculation didn't include the costs to the company of not taking action on business development activities during this time.

This is only one small example of how companies suffer from a lack of consciousness or presence. When a leader becomes conscious, of their inner world first, then how they lead, they can literally transform their team or company into a productive, engaged, and innovative group of people working toward a common goal.

THE OPPORTUNITY OF PRESENCE

After reading the earlier section on costs, it's no surprise that many studies show American workers' stress levels are at an all time high, health is declining, and satisfaction with our lives is at an all time low. Not being present or staying unconscious isn't working. The great news is these painful costs can be transformed through the practice of presence.

If you're like many people I've worked with, you are going to be skeptical of what I have to say in this section. You will think it sounds too good to be true, or that it might work for others, but not for your highly specific situation. I know how you're feeling because I was there, too. I didn't start believing until I saw results for myself. Since my years of experimenting with presence, I have transformed my health, deepened my marriage, become a stronger parent, and expanded my creativity not to mention my business's bottom line. I have never made more money and been healthier and happier (all at the same time) in my life. My clients' experiences and my own have been consistent. When you become present in your daily life you gain access to information, data, hunches, and thoughts that will guide your life, career, or company to new levels of success and enjoyment.

Although these results are wonderful and often life-changing for my clients, they aren't the reason people hire me in the first place. Leaders hire me because they want to strengthen their presence (how they are perceived by others) or because they have hit a plateau in their leadership career and don't know why. Essentially, they are feeling the pain of "what got you here, won't get you there."

One of my clients was a newly appointed general manager for a TV station. The stagnant station was drawn to his big vision and stellar record for making things happen, and those skills moved him up the career ladder quickly. But as he started his new role, he was faced with immediate resistance. The harder he tried to make things happen, the worse the staff reacted. Three months into the job, he was facing a potential coup. He was flabbergasted and at a loss as to how to move forward. Everything he knew to do to make the station "better" wasn't working, and worse yet, it was backfiring on him.

By the time I was brought in, the GM was in the midst of some serious "pain," and his work situation had gotten his attention in a big way. He was ready to listen and try anything. As we began to work together, it was obvious he was brilliant at the business of building a station, but his mind was moving so fast, that it was also obvious he was incompetent at being present. He wasn't paying attention to the signs people were giving him, to the culture he was entering, or to the fact that his direct reports were frustrated. He was astounded to hear how much I picked up on in one, one-hour meeting that he had failed to notice during the previous several months. This may sound like an extreme case, but it happens all the time. We miss out on vital information when we're not present.

Some of the most consistent and compelling reasons leaders and companies invest in strengthening their ability to be present are:

• **Compelling Leadership Presence:** When you're in the company of someone who is truly present, you know it. You can feel it. When you invest in your ability to be present in the moment, your personal presence strengthens. Unconsciously people are drawn to that strength and naturally want to follow. Leaders who have strengthened their presence muscle are strong, resilient, open, authentic, intuitive, and flexible.

• **Increased Efficiency:** The ability to be present allows you to respond to demands effectively and initiate the most effective action in the right time. You will experience higher levels of productivity, less rework, fewer mistakes, fewer "misses," and more precision in your execution.

• **Improved Innovation:** The ability to be present requires you to engage both sides of your brain-your objective and linear side, as well as your sensing, creative, and intuitive side. When you experiment more with presence, you will feel more creative and gain access to a higher level of problem solving. You will have more innovative ideas come to you in the most unexpected ways, seemingly out of the blue.

• **Ease:** When you are present with your gut feelings, thoughts, and emotions, it gives you a sense of being "in the flow." You will experience effortlessness in your work, getting more done, yet feeling as if you worked less hard.

The longer you practice and experiment with presence, the more results you'll experience. Reducing stress is often the first benefit people experience from practicing presence, and operating from a place of less stress immediately improves results. So, really you can't go wrong with giving presence a try.

BONUS BENEFITS OF PRESENCE

When you raise your consciousness, it has a ripple effect. Very seldom will you consciously know how far-reaching that impact is.

Benefits to You

As you engage with presence, you will feel an immediate sense of clarity. Your perspective about your challenges will change; you will feel more resourceful and creative about how you approach your work and life.

The pressure and stress you feel will give way to a sense of purpose and hope about your future. Instead of having to "power your way through," you will likely experience more synchronicities and things "falling into place." Life will feel easier.

You will know a greater sense of perspective. You'll feel less reactive. Life will make more sense to you, and your priorities may shift. You may decide to work less hard and get better results.

You will be healthier, make more money, and become better looking. I can't make promises on these, but I've seen all of this happen more than once! Don't underestimate the attractiveness of presence.

Benefits to Those You Lead

As your presence strengthens those you lead will immediately take notice. They may have a hard time articulating the change, but they *will* notice. They will relax into your leadership and naturally trust you more. They will feel inspired to follow you and have more confidence in your decisions. They will want to back you up and rally the troops to follow your lead. Your leadership will become more compelling and infectious. Your experience of leading others will be more fun, and you'll feel less pressure that can emerge when you are responsible for leading others.

You will be able to ask more from your team and get them to deliver. If they can't or are unwilling to deliver, you will take bold action without hesitating. Everyone wants to be in the presence of a strong leader. When one is present, we breathe a little easier, rest a little more, and are inspired to follow.

Benefits to Your World

Not only will you and those you lead feel better, more motivated, and purposeful, but your presence will inspire those around you, often without you knowing it. When someone with a strong presence enters a room, people can feel it and are inspired. As you engage with your family, friends, and communities, they will feel the power of your solidness. That alone can be transforming for people. When you are in the grocery store or at soccer games and other public events, don't underestimate the power of your eye contact, warmth, and strength. Your energy *will* touch others in ways you can't and won't comprehend.

As you go further along the path with this ongoing work, you will gain greater clarity about your purpose and undoubtedly move leaps and bounds toward fulfilling it. When you are living your true purpose, there is nothing that is of greater service to the whole of humanity.

CHAPTER 2:

(THE FOUNDATION OF)
PRESENCE

"Between stimulus and response there is a space. In that space is our power to choose our response. In our response lies our growth and our freedom."

—Victor E. Frankl

WHEN MY CLIENTS BEGIN actively practicing being present, every one of them at some point "confesses" that they noticed they weren't truly paying attention in a meeting, or weren't present for a day, or even most of the week. I assure them this is normal, and I point out that the fact they even noticed is an act of presence. The goal of presence isn't perfection, and in fact, that's not possible for most of us. The goal in your practice of presence is to simply pay attention on purpose as often as you can. The moment you notice you're not paying attention, you've just become a bit more present.

The two key factors you need to build a strong foundation to be successful in practicing presence are your mind and your body. Understanding and working with your mind and body alone will not only help you strengthen your presence, but they will give context to your reactions in all aspects of your life. Any moves you make to build a strong foundation will immediately make you feel better.

THE PRESENCE TUG OF WAR

We already know it's hard to maintain presence because our attention is pulled in so many directions, but that's not the only battle we face in trying to maintain presence. There is a constant tug of war taking place, and it's happening in your brain. When learning about the practice of presence, it's imperative that you understand this tug of war so you can learn to work with it and not against it. There's a part of our brain that is constantly scanning the environment for danger, and its purpose is survival and protection. This part of your brain is called the Amygdala.

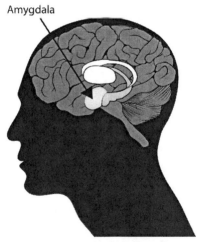

Amygdala

In popular psychology, there are other names for this part of our brain, including "monkey mind," "the gremlin," "reptilian brain," "primordial brain," and "ego."

The Amygdala is the primal functioning part of our brain. It is responsible for our fight-or-flight responses. As information from the outside world comes in, it is first unconsciously filtered through your Amygdala.

The Amygdala determines if something you're experiencing is (or will be) a threat based on your past experiences and emotional memories. If it determines the situation you're in is a threat, it will take action without you having to think about it, thus operating unconsciously.

I was conducting a training class on candid communication in the workplace, and Susan, a participant, asked why she feels so "amped" when she even thinks about entering into a tough conversation. She shared that she can feel her heart race, her neck and chest get warm, and she held up her fists to demonstrate how she was feeling. She admitted that it doesn't really make sense that she would be so amped, because most of the people she works with are reasonable people. What Susan was experiencing, however, was the unconscious physiological response of her Amygdala being activated.

When your Amygdala determines that something you are experiencing or are going to experience is a threat, it activates your body's natural stress response, which includes an increase in blood volume, rise in blood pressure, increase in blood glucose, and release of a hormone called Cortisol to help you physically move fast. This is called the sympathetic nervous system, and it's designed to get us out of danger quickly without having to think about it. This part of our brain was incredibly helpful when we were faced with a kind of physical danger we can't imagine today. Imagine facing predators like saber-toothed cats. Our ability to quickly take action (like running) without "thinking" about it was imperative to our survival as a species.

THE FOUNDATION OF YOUR MIND

As we have evolved as a species, we are not faced with as much physical danger as our ancestors were. Instead our Amygdalas are constantly scanning for twenty-first century threats that are usually emotional and social in nature. This primal part of our brain is scanning for situations that could cause emotional pain or cause us to lose social status. The Amygdala uses past emotional memories to determine if something is a threat. Essentially, it's constantly scanning the environment for potential pain. When I asked Susan about her past experience with stressful conversations, she recalled that most resulted in conflict, and that she had learned at an early age that conflict was negative and painful. That emotional memory is firmly imprinted in Susan's Amygdala, and even though she's not being faced with a physical threat, her Amygdala remembers the pain conflict caused in her past. Even though today she's a strong adult, her body and mind unconsciously respond to the potential pain of a tough conversation, and she prepares by activating her "fight" response.

The primary focus of your Amygdala is to

keep you alive and safe. It's easier for it to do that when you maintain the status quo and stick with your habits and predictable routines. Essentially when you operate from your unconscious patterns and aren't really present, your Amygdala gets to call the shots. You staying unconscious is a win for your Amygdala, simply because it's easier to keep you safe. For your Amygdala, predictability equals safety.

As a leader, it's not really in your DNA to maintain the status quo for too long. You like to expand, learn new things, and take risks. The part of you that thinks objectively, is willing to take risks, and try new things is located in a different part of your brain called the pre-frontal cortex, or frontal lobe.

Your frontal lobe is responsible for expressing language, impulse control, objectivity, empathy, humor, flexibility, judgment, and complex problem solving. When you use this more sophisticated part of your brain, you are able to accurately assess danger and threats from a more

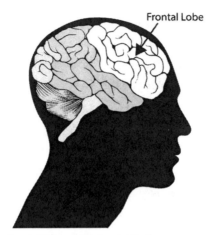

Frontal Lobe

Frontal Lobe or Pre-Frontal Cortex

objective place, not from a place of past emotional experience, which is what your Amygdala
does. The responses of your Amygdala are not
very sophisticated. They are more like the responses of a child who hasn't learned about life
yet. Your frontal lobe's responses are more like
those of a mature adult who has had a lot of life
experience and uses those experiences and skills
to make effective decisions, including how and
when to take risks.

When you engage in something new or surprising, or you attempt to expand your skillsets or knowledge base by choice, your Amygdala gets triggered and your body responds accordingly. For example, recently I joined a new dance class, and I could feel my Amygdala response kick in. As I entered the studio my body got tense, my heart was pounding, and I started to worry I might not be able to keep up. Because of my triggered state, my body was tense and not as fluid, so I didn't dance as well as I am able to. It may not have made "logical" sense that I was nervous, since I feel supported and safe at my studio and it was my choice to attend the new class, but the Amygdala doesn't operate based on logic. It uses emotional memories as a way to filter experiences.

Here's another example of how the Amygdala uses past emotional memories and how it can unconsciously hijack your leadership. Lori, the VP of marketing at a financial services firm, came to me with a desire to interact more effectively with her peers, because she was feeling shut out by them. All of her peers and her boss were male. When we talked through her typical reactions it was clear she was a "fighter," not someone who flees or shuts down. We talked through how upsetting it felt to her to feel shut out and how she ended up coming to every meeting feeling on edge, waiting to hear yet another decision she didn't get to be a part of. I regularly observe my clients leading or participating in meetings, and when I observed her, it was clear that she engaged in meetings with her Amygdala fully activated. She walked into meetings literally prepared for a fight-and guess what? She found one every time. She was aware there was a problem, and she could feel her body tensing up, she just didn't know how to stop the pattern of behavior. There was no way she could effectively interact with her peers as long as she was unconscious to the source of her triggers. Knowing the Amygdala is the home of our emotional memories, I was curious about what Lori's Amygdala was reacting to. I asked her if she could remember a time when

she was in a similar situation—maybe not as lit-
eral as sitting around a table with a bunch of men
who weren't listening to her, but a time when she
felt similar feelings. After a bit she smiled at me
and said, "Oh my gosh, I can't believe this. It's exactly how I felt around the dinner table with my
three older brothers and my parents. They were
always talking about their lives, and they never
listened to me. I always felt like the little sister
who didn't know anything." Bingo! There it was-
the emotional memory she wasn't conscious of,
but her Amygdala remembered and was trying to
protect her from feeling that pain again.

What's important to remember about the
Amygdala is that it tries to protect us from a le-
gitimate pain by creating some way to cope or
compensate. That initial response is usually helpful. In Lori's case, she learned at a young age that
the only way to be heard by her older brothers
was to speak up and insert herself in the conversation. Over time, we need to learn that the
behavior that helped us when we were younger

eventually starts backfiring and tends to create the very thing we don't want to experience. Lori's Amygdala didn't want her to experience the pain of being left out again, but her "fight" responses alienated her peers and her defensiveness essentially caused them to *want* to avoid her. For Lori, her Amygdala was only remembering what it felt like to be young, left out, and out of control. Once we could identify the unconscious trigger, she was immediately freed to take more control of her destiny. Understanding her trigger allowed her to move into her frontal lobe, and she could then consciously choose her behaviors and communicate more collaboratively. After a few months with this understanding and presence, all of her peers reported Lori was much easier to work with, and importantly, she felt she was a part of the team.

WORKING WITH YOUR AMYGDALA

When your Amygdala has been triggered, your objectivity and resourcefulness is nowhere to be found. For example, think back to a time when you were in a heated argument or surprised by something and responded by either fighting with the person or shutting down. Then only after you were out of the situation did it dawn on you that you should have done or said something else that would have been more constructive. Hindsight is often 20/20, not only because you learn from experience, but the clarity also comes from your Amygdala no longer being triggered. It takes the Amygdala .85 seconds to react, but it takes your body nearly twenty minutes to recover from the physiological impact of your Amygdala being triggered.

The goal in working with the Amygdala is to move away from being unconscious to becoming the objective *observer*. Just as if you are watching a movie, you want to be able to disconnect from making the reactions mean something about you, and rather simply observe or watch when the Amygdala is activated.

When developing your ability to be present, it's helpful to observe how your Amygdala typically responds. We know the Amygdala will use a fight-or-flight response when triggered, but let's look a little deeper at how your Amygdala responds to situations it deems dangerous.

Remember, your Amygdala loves predictability and control, and its purpose is to "protect" you from pain. It gets triggered when it senses you don't have control in a situation, and as a result, it will express itself in two ways—internally and externally. As a way of gaining control and thus protecting you, it will turn on other people and cause you to go on the attack. Or if it feels gaining control will be costly, it will turn inward on you, making you retreat.

The following charts highlight behaviors you can observe to help you discover whether your Amygdala is expressing itself externally and/or internally.

Your Amygdala is expressing itself externally if you behave in any of these ways:

- Competing
- Condescending behavior
- One-upping
- Acting superior
- Passive-aggressive behavior
- Power plays
- Stone-walling or refusing to talk
- Name calling
- "CYA" behavior
- I win/you lose mentality
- "Prove it to me" behavior
- Quick to criticize others
- Pissing contests
- Defensiveness
- Talking over people/ interrupting
- Railroading a conversation
- Posturing
- Yelling or swearing
- Inflexible or rigid
- Us vs. Them mentality

What's the most common way your Amygdala expresses itself externally?

_____

_____

_____

_____

_____

_____

Your Amygdala is expressing itself internally if you behave in any of these ways:

- Self-doubt or "imposter syndrome"
- Feeling stuck
- Need to prove oneself or "show value"
- It's "all or nothing" feeling
- Procrastination
- Feeling that others are out to get you
- Perfectionism
- Feeling that you don't have support
- You over-work and/or don't promote yourself and your achievements
- Telling yourself you need to "toughen up" or "get over it"
- Lack of holding good boundaries
- Worrying about the past
- Trouble saying "no"
- Feeling better/less than someone else
- Feeling like you have no choice
- Comparing yourself to others
- Addiction to compliments/ feedback
- Feeling like a victim
- Worrying about the future
- Taking other people's actions personally

What's the most common way your Amygdala expresses itself internally?

_____

_____

_____

_____

_____

_____

_____

_____

When your Amygdala feels threatened or out of control, it will turn in on you or outward onto others, or both. The intention of observing the responses of your Amygdala is that it will give you data and inevitably help you become more present. Paying attention to your responses will help you wake up to your unconscious behavior. But before you can change your behavior, you first need to become conscious of it.

The next step is to get curious about the _source_ of the triggering. For Lori, the source of her trigger was the feeling of being the "little sister that no one listened to." Identifying the source can be a bit harder to do on your own because your Amygdala won't be too keen on you figuring this out. Remember, the more you stay unconscious, the easier it is for your Amygdala to protect you, so as you go through this exercise, pay attention to your responses, both physically and mentally, as they may give you information. Don't worry if you can't identify the source right away. Declaring your intention to know the source is great forward movement in becoming more conscious.

Exercise:

Write down a situation at work or home in which your reaction wasn't constructive or helpful. Ideally, it would be a situation/reaction that you've experienced more than once. It could be with the same people or even better, different people. We're looking for a pattern if possible.

_____

_____

_____

_____

_____

_____

_____

_____

_____

_____

_____

_____

Now, answer these questions as best you can:

1. What was the surface issue that caused you to react? (i.e., my wife didn't listen, my peer didn't keep their word, I was blamed for something I didn't do)

_____

_____

_____

_____

_____

_____

_____

_____

_____

_____

_____

_____

2. What do you think your Amygdala was trying to protect you from? (i.e., being alone, looking bad, losing my job)

_____

_____

_____

_____

_____

_____

_____

_____

_____

_____

_____

3. Does this situation remind you of a similar situation from your past? (This doesn't have to necessarily be from your childhood.)

_____

_____

_____

_____

_____

_____

_____

_____

_____

_____

_____

4. If you had to guess, what is the source of this particular trigger?

_____

_____

_____

_____

_____

_____

_____

_____

_____

_____

_____

_____

These questions are designed to help you look a bit deeper and gain more understanding of your responses but know that having the "story" isn't absolutely necessary in working with your Amygdala. Simply noticing your responses and even having an understanding of your most common triggers is all you need to start building a strong foundation for presence.

THE FOUNDATION OF YOUR BODY

When you understand the presence tug of war and what the Amygdala response feels like in your body, you are set up to be more successful in bringing yourself back to presence. Like in the example of my Amygdala getting triggered in my new dance class, the awareness of my body's reaction alone gave me data that a part of me was feeling threatened. I was able to tune into my body's responses well before my mind could identify the "story." Because our minds and bodies are so connected, we can use one or the other as a doorway into presence. In my dance class, I didn't have time (nor interest, really) to analyze the source of my trigger. All I needed was the awareness that my body was reacting to cue me to calm down and come back into my frontal lobe and truly enjoy the class. The beauty of the human brain is that with practice, we are able to fluidly move between our unconscious and conscious parts, and often just tuning into our bodies and their responses is all we need to cue us.

Your ability to be present and pay attention is highly dependent on the state of your physical body. This is one of the first places I go when working with a new client. Because of busy schedules, travel, and the demands of life, it's common for leaders to forfeit the basics like eating, sleeping, and exercising. When you overlook your physical needs, you are less able to stay in your frontal lobe and be resilient, and you're a lot more likely to spiral into an Amygdala reaction.

Your Amygdala evolved to help you survive, so when you are hungry, thirsty, or tired your Amygdala goes on high alert. Neither your mind nor your body operates at its full capacity when you are tired, hungry, or thirsty, and yet the act of taking care of our basic needs tends to be the first thing to go out the window when we become busy.

Let's take a deeper look into how the foundation of your body supports or detracts from your ability to be resilient and present.

Blood Sugar: Blood sugar or glucose levels in your brain keep it active and alert. When your glucose levels drop, your body is essentially hungry for energy. If you ignore it and skip a meal or snack, you are setting yourself up for an Amygdala reaction. I know this is true for me and my husband because the time we tend to argue with one another is right before dinner when we're tired from the day and hungry. Eating three meals a day, including protein and fiber, as well as two to three snacks between meals will help you maintain your blood sugar and prevent an Amygdala hijack.

Hydration: In a study published in the December 2012 issue of *The Journal of Nutrition*[2] researchers found that dehydration was a prime factor in causing headaches, loss of focus, fatigue, and bad mood. I also read that dehydration negatively impacts the executive functions of your brain located in your pre-frontal cortex, the part of your brain that allows you to think objectively and problem solve. If your pre-frontal cortex or frontal lobe is impaired, it's much more likely your Amygdala will take over. Although scientists still argue over just how much water is good for you, the general rule is six to eight glasses of water a day will keep your brain and body hydrated and that helps set the stage for you to think more objectively. If nothing else, start your day with one big glass of water, because we lose water while we sleep, thus we start our day dehydrated. Enjoy your coffee, right after your water!

Sleep: A study performed at the University of Pennsylvania states that inadequate sleep increases perceived stress and negative effect in response to relatively easy tasks[3]. The bottom line is, the less sleep you get, the less resourceful you become and the less present you'll be. Of course it's ideal to get seven to eight hours of sleep each night, so trying to go to bed earlier, even if only by fifteen minutes will be a win for creating a strong foundation for your presence.

The foundation of presence is your awareness of how much your body—your brain in particular—can run the show without you being conscious of it. Becoming aware of your Amygdala, its typical triggers and responses can transform your ability to be present. By understanding the brain science behind your reactions and the foundation of what your body needs in terms of food, water, and sleep, you will be set up to be in the driver's seat on your road to presence.

Here's a recap of some simple strategies to help make your foundation even stronger:

- Make a list of your most common triggers and try to anticipate them before they happen.

- If you are triggered, try to create a "pause" just for a moment such as taking a deep breath, taking a drink of water, or trying to feel your feet on the floor. Use the pause to see if you can move into your frontal lobe while your body calms down.

- Just for one week, start your day off with a glass of water, then have one before lunch and one before dinner. Three extra glasses of water will not only help keep you hydrated, but will also prevent you from over-eating.

- This weekend shop for a few easy snacks to have at the office like healthy granola bars (Kashi are my favorite), nuts, fruits, or even hard-boiled eggs, cheese, or yogurt. Put an appointment in your calendar between 3 to 4 pm to remind yourself to eat a snack.

- Three nights next week see if you can go to bed fifteen minutes earlier than normal. A stretch goal would be thirty minutes, but anything will help!

CHAPTER 3:

(PRACTICING PRESENCE)

"Sometimes the most important thing in a whole day is the rest we take between two deep breaths."

—Etty Hillesum

THIS CHAPTER IS FOCUSED on simple strategies to help you return to presence. Some of them, at first glance, may appear to be rudimentary or overly simplified, but don't be fooled. Although the tools are simple in concept, the application isn't always easy, and therein lies the practice. The best way to work with this chapter is to read through all of the tools and exercises and identify two that you feel most inspired to try. Then experiment with those tools for a week or two, and come back and add to your repertoire.

I encourage you to observe your reaction when you experiment with the exercises and tools. No need to judge your reaction, just notice. The first goal, always, is to simply be the observer of your responses and to remember that the simple act of observing is the strongest position for you to be able to return to the place of presence. At some point I expect you'll hit up against an area that your mind or body doesn't want to go. When that happens, don't force it; yet don't back away. See if you can just be with the tension, simply observe and see what happens. Often simply being with the reaction is the fastest way for it to transform. Wrestling with the tension, on the other hand, only strengthens the resistance.

You may notice a theme in these tools. None of them should feel "hard." In fact, the act of returning to presence creates a sense of ease and joy. Many of my clients feel guilty or think they are getting away with something when they experiment with these tools because it doesn't feel like "work." The beautiful thing about presence is that because it's our natural state, coming back to it feels good. The only trick is simply to observe your thoughts when your mind wants to make you feel guilty or tell you that you don't have "time" for these exercises.

As you read through this chapter keep in mind that you can use any of the tools as "triage," or ways to help you calm down and get grounded again when you're feeling triggered. You can also use them as preventative tools that add to your level of resilience and sense of joy. The great news is that none of these take a lot of time; instead they just require you to experiment with them with intention. In fact, many of the tools can be practiced during your normal day. For example, you can transform the way you enjoy meals by being really present with what and how you're eating. Even taking a shower in the morning can be used as a practice. The leaders I work with are busy and don't need another thing on their "to do" lists, and I imagine you are similar.

The process I take my clients through to build their presence muscle starts by looking at the foundation of their schedule and physical needs. Then we move to ways they can leverage the wisdom of their mind and heart. The reason I start with the basics of one's schedule and body is because, without the foundation of having some space and meeting one's physical needs, returning to presence is just plain difficult, if not impossible. If your schedule is out of control or your body is not getting what it needs, you won't be able to access the wisdom the rest of your system has to offer. Even if you have your schedule and body's needs taken care of, I invite you to read through these sections anyway to see if you might be able to amplify your already successful practices.

GATEWAY #1: YOUR SCHEDULE

In my first session with one of my clients, the CEO of a mid-sized public real-estate company, I asked him to talk me through his schedule during his last two weeks. What I noticed is that nearly every day he was in back-to-back meetings, on email early in the morning and late in the evening (after his kids went to bed), and his weekends were packed with family commitments. He was tired, yet had a hard time letting down, and it was clear his schedule was not sustainable. He agreed with my observation, but the thought of making a change seemed daunting.

Most of my clients' schedules are packed full with back-to-back meetings, travel, and tight deadlines, and few of them feel they have much control over their schedule. When I push back on their thinking a bit, they see where they can make a change. The art of building a schedule that works isn't always easy, but some of the following practices can help you get there.

Build in Transition Time

So many leaders are in back-to-back meetings without taking a break. This stresses the adrenal system and the Amygdala is more likely to react. I ask my clients to build in transition times between meetings, and as they shift from one kind of activity to another. Almost all of them at first say, "I don't think I can do that because I don't set the meeting time." That's fine, but what can you do to build a little more space? Can you set the expectation at the beginning of the meeting that you will be leaving five minutes early? Can you start your next meeting five or ten minutes past the hour? Ideally, can you set up fifteen minutes of transition time between your meetings?

Then, when you create a little transition time, use it intentionally. Notice how your body is feeling. You might need to use the restroom, eat a snack, or get a cup of tea. You might remember a detail that needs your attention. Use the time to take a few deep breaths and set yourself up for success at your next meeting. Several years ago I observed a meeting at Microsoft being led by a corporate vice president. The conference room was packed with about twenty-five people, and one chair at the head of the table was empty while everyone eagerly awaited that person's arrival. It was a high-stakes meeting, but I was still surprised by how much tension there was in the room even before the meeting began. The leader was eight minutes late, and when he walked in, it was obvious he had been rushing to get to the meeting as he was breathing heavily. He walked into the room with his back to the participants, put his things down, and took a deep breath. He sat down, looked around the room, and smiled at everyone and in his charming British accent said, "Did you know Sesame Street is thinking about getting rid of the cookie monster?" This leader used his one minute of transition time masterfully by taking a deep breath and becoming present. In a short amount of time, he brought himself to presence, got a feel for who was in the room, and broke the tension. This is a masterful example of a leader, who had little control over his schedule, yet leveraged his presence to lead more effectively.

PRACTICE: Look at your schedule with the assumption you have some control to build time in to transition between meetings. Ask for what you need from others (like adjusting the meeting time or length) or at minimum, intentionally leverage the little bit of time you do have to become present.

Create "White Space" Time

My former business partner, Michele Christensen and I used the term white space time to describe a chunk of time you have reserved that does not have a predetermined agenda. This means that you block out time (ideally 1-4 hours a week) and you don't know how you're going to use the time until you begin. The purpose of white space time is quite simple. It's space for you to give yourself whatever you need, but the point is not to decide what you need until you begin.

When you begin your white space time, you simply ask yourself, "What do I need right now?" or "What is it that I'm inspired to do?" Leaders rarely have time to think, so many of my clients use their white space time to become present and turn their attention to simply thinking about whatever situation needs their attention. Others use white space time to not think, but to simply be, and at different times they use their time to treat themselves, attend to important details they wouldn't normally have time for, or even take a nap. When you enter into your white space time and ask yourself "What do I need right now?" your answer may surprise you. Many of my clients don't realize how tired they are until they start their white space time. Others tune in and realize they are starving for some peace and quiet, so they go and take a walk outside.

One of my clients, a president of a design company, told me that he starts his white space time with a walk around a local university's campus located near his office. Seeing the big trees and beautiful buildings inspires him and helps him get present. After just a few minutes, he gets clarity about what he needs and then uses the next ninety minutes to focus on that. In a matter of six weeks, he developed what turned out to be the company's most innovative and profitable business plan to date. He admitted to me that he would never have created something so innovative without having the white space time to think through it.

PRACTICE: Create some white space time in your calendar. Can you find an hour during the week? It doesn't always have to be during business hours. You could always use an evening or weekend, too. Getting started is the hardest part; so find an hour this week and next week and block it now. Then after that, book a regular time each week that works for your schedule. You may have to end up scheduling over it, but it will remind you to find a different time during the week to give yourself white space time.

Use Travel Time Wisely

Many of my clients travel frequently and under-estimate the toll it takes on them. The act of arriving at the airport, getting through security, flying for hours, and then arriving to your final destination takes a lot of energy. No matter how easy the trip might be, traveling literally un-grounds you. It's no wonder that returning to a state of presence is even harder when you're on the road. I'm all for efficiency, but I'm not a fan of my clients working up until the last minute before they have to go to the airport, working on the plane, and then getting back on their computers when they arrive at their hotel. Instead, I encourage you to use your travel time wisely. Here's a list of best practices while traveling that will help you make the most out of your time away from home.

• **Don't go to the office before you fly.** Work from home before you fly or better yet, use the time before the trip to create a little bit more space for yourself to do whatever you want.

• **Prepare to eat well.** Bring good food with you on the plane so you're not prisoner to bad plane food.

• **Use flying time as white space.** Don't automatically open your laptop and start working, instead, ask yourself what you really need. Maybe a little nap or time to unwind and watch a movie or read would be more helpful?

• **Treat yourself.** When you arrive to your hotel, treat yourself to something you don't normally get to do, (i.e. watch a good show, take a long shower or bath, or order room service).

• **Steward your energy.** Give yourself permission to skip the social event at the end of the day, or at minimum leave it a bit early.

It's tempting to not pay attention to your energy when you're on the road, but by not paying attention you aren't at your best, and worse yet, you have to pay for the lack of energy when you return. You will gain both immediate and long-term benefits by using your travel time just a bit more wisely.

GATEWAY #2: YOUR BODY

The body may be one of my favorite and most reliable gateways for bringing myself back into presence. Not only do these body related practices get me out of my head, they are also enjoyable, relaxing, and healthy for my body and mind.

As I discussed earlier, using the body as a gateway to presence is also among the easiest things to forget. When stress kicks in and the Amygdala is activated, we lose our focus on the very thing that would help us the most. In times of mounting stress, experimenting with these tools may feel counter-logical, but it's during these very times that nourishing the body is most beneficial and allows you to operate from your wiser self more quickly.

Activate Your Senses

We are sensual beings by nature, and our senses provide part of the richness and joy of life. Just think back to when you watched a beautiful sunset, enjoyed a delicious meal, heard a song that moved you, or took a hot shower that reenergized you. If you wonder if our senses are really that important, take a look at what people post on Facebook. How many people post pictures of a beautiful meal, sunset, or about the songs they're listening to? Our senses can move us, inspire us, and best of all, our senses can bring us to the present moment.

Here's a list of some ways you can use your senses to bring you into presence:

• **Really pay attention to what and how you're eating.** Notice what your food looks like before you eat it, smell it, pay attention to the texture and flavor in your mouth. Eating with presence not only helps you enjoy a meal, but you might also notice that your body is full more quickly and eat less as a result!

- **Look at something beautiful.** Getting outside is the best way to utilize this sense, but even if you can't escape your office, take a look at a picture of a past vacation or of a loved one. The homepage for the search engine Bing posts a different and beautiful picture every day. Also simply looking at something green (preferably a tree or plant) calms your nervous system.

- **Keep something that smells great at your desk.** That could be flowers, some nice lotion to rub on your hands, or essential oils. I always provide organic lavender stress balls at any offsite meeting I facilitate. It not only keeps people's hand busy, but it emits just enough lavender to help calm their system.

- **Listen.** I can't stress enough how the act of simply listening can bring you into the present moment.

The next time you're engaged in a conversation, try to listen without thinking about what you're going to say next. Listen to great music or the sounds outside. Even better, try to be in silence, and listen to the subtle sounds that you hear like the clock ticking or the sound of the wind. Even a few minutes of really listening can transform your experience of the present.

• **Enjoy the sense of touch.** When I'm out and about I love touching things I see to feel their texture. The sense of touch can be activated anytime and can help bring you into presence. Enjoy the feeling of washing your hands, holding a warm coffee cup, putting on a warm pair of socks, hugging someone you care about, or petting your animal. You can even just pay attention to the feeling of your clothes against your body.

Your senses are there to provide you a gateway to presence and joy. By simply tuning into

them you will strengthen your presence muscle
and I suspect will enjoy the process too.

Movement

Do you find yourself having to sit for long peri-
ods of time? Do you forfeit your favorite exercise so you can get a little more work done? If
so, you're not alone, and the lack of movement
can take a toll on your body and mental state.
Movement, no matter what kind, helps move
the stagnate energy in your body to bring more
clarity and energy, and it supports your ability to
stay present in the moment. You'll benefit all day
from movement or exercise you engage in during
the morning hours.

Exercise of any kind is considered movement,
so if you have a regular exercise regime, con-
gratulations! I'm not one of those people who's
ever really enjoyed exercise, but boy do I wish I
was. I have experimented with dozens of forms
of movement, and the bottom line for me is that

I have to enjoy it. The moment it feels like exercise is the moment I can't stand it. I consider each of the activities listed below as "moving meditation" because not only am I moving my body, I also feel more connected to my inner wisdom as a result of engaging in the movement. Here's a list of my favorite ways to move my body that doesn't feel like traditional exercise:

- **Yoga.** I love how good my body feels after yoga. For me, the power of yoga helps me connect internally, and it improves my ability to be present.

- **Pilates.** I have a private Pilates session each week, and as much as it hurts sometimes, I always feel happy about being there. It helps me connect deeper into my core both physically and mentally. I always walk out of the studio feeling more clear and strong.

- **Dance.** I'm a dancer at heart and have recently competed in ballroom dancing, but I gave up the gowns for the bare feet of modern dance. I've also been known to blast the music and have a spontaneous dance party (mainly by myself), especially when I'm stuck. I highly recommend Michael Jackson's "Wanna Be Starting Something."

- **Golf.** I don't think about much other than golf when I'm on the course, so not only is it a great practice in presence, but I'm walking, swinging (a lot!), and taking in the beautiful outdoors.

- **Hiking.** There's nothing better than hiking a new trail with my family and dog, getting my heart rate up, and finding new natural treasures we've never seen before.

- **Yard work or cleaning.** Yes, it's true; I love to clean—inside or outside the house. If you do it with some vigor, you'll be sweating in no time, and I swear to you, some of my best business ideas have come to me while my hands are busy.

- **Swimming.** There's something really magical about water for me, especially if it's a natural body of water like a lake or ocean. Anytime I have the chance, I love to move my body by swimming.

- **Playing.** Believe it or not, some of the best and most fun ways of moving my body include playing tag, soccer, or "monkey in the middle" with my boys. We run, get a little competitive, and inevitably end up in a good belly laugh by the end. It's so good for all of our bodies and souls.

There are dozens of other ways to move your body, and there's no "right" way. There are a variety of ways I move my body each week, and I encourage you to do the same.

When you don't have time to engage in an hour-long adventure, here are some quick ways you can get your energy flowing in five minutes or less:

- **Airplane arms.** Stand with your legs hip-width apart with your arms straight out like an airplane. While breathing in, twist at your waist to one side so one of your arms is in front of you, while the other is in back. On your exhale, switch by twisting your waist and arms to the other side. Do this for five to ten breaths, and you should feel more energized.

- **Rub hands together.** Between meetings or during a break, simply rub your hands together vigorously until you can't stand the heat. Really put your energy into it and notice how your hands, arms, and back tingle with the movement of energy.

- **Legs up the wall.** If you can find a wall and have a moment, sit facing the wall, and then move your tailbone as close to the wall as you can. Then lie down and put your legs up the wall so the backs of your legs are on the wall. You may have to scoot a bit closer to the wall, but the idea is to allow the wall to support your legs. The inversion of your legs helps move your energy throughout your body.

• **Bending over at the waist.** A quick way to help move stagnate energy is to bend forward at the waist and let your arms dangle. While you're bent over, simply take in a few deep breaths and let the air out. This is both calming and energizing at the same time.

Breathing

Deep breathing is one of the best ways to lower stress in the body. When you breathe deeply, it sends a message to your brain to calm down and relax. The brain then sends this message to your body. Those things that happen when you are stressed, such as increased heart rate, fast breathing, and high blood pressure, all decrease as you breathe deeply to relax. Many clients tell me they count to ten and breathe when they have been triggered as a way to calm down and prevent themselves from saying something they may regret. If you have a practice that includes breathing, that's fantastic. Here are a few more breathing techniques that may help you calm down, transition between meetings, or just simply help bring your focus to the present.

- **Three conscious breaths.** The Dalai Lama says that just three conscious breaths can help you come into a conscious state. It can be as simple as that. When you are feeling stressed, stuck in your head, or triggered, try to take three conscious breaths. Take a slow, deep inhalation through your nose without force, and then hold for a second, and slowly release the breath through your mouth. Repeat two more times or more if you feel inspired.

- **Focus on the in and out.** If you have only five minutes, simply closing your eyes and focusing on your breathing can profoundly shift your stress level and help you access your deeper wisdom. As you breathe for five minutes, your mind will naturally drift, thoughts will come in and out, and you'll likely feel as if you're doing it wrong. The point isn't to be free of thought, the point is to simply observe the thoughts and not become attached to them as they pass by the screen of your mind. A way to help focus your practice is to simply focus on the in and out of your breath. When you breathe in, think "in." When you breathe out, think "out." This helps you stay in the present moment with your breath, and eventually your mind may settle down. If it doesn't, that's okay too. The point is to simply practice the presence of breath.

- **Breath of fire.** The "Breath of Fire" (BOF) technique is one of the foundational breathing exercises used in Kundalini Yoga. According to Kudalini-Yoga-Info.com, the Breath of Fire technique is an effective way to balance and strengthen the nervous system, stimulate the solar plexus to release natural energy throughout the body, and help you gain control in a stressful situation. Do this technique by pumping the navel point in and out while breathing rapidly through the nose. Breathe through the nostrils with the mouth closed; your breaths in and out are of equal lengths. While practicing this technique, the body stays relatively relaxed and the navel works vigorously pulling in toward your spine on the exhalation. As you first start to practice BOF, lay on the floor to check that your breathing is correct. Put your hand over your belly button, and when you inhale, your hand should rise; when you exhale your hand should move down toward your spine. The more practiced you become, the faster the breath can travel. Practicing BOF for just a few minutes can immediately improve your energy level and nervous system.

GATEWAY #3: YOUR HEART

Your heart houses some of your deepest wisdom, including your creativity, caring, empathy, and compassion. In 1994, scientist J.A. Armour from the University of Montreal determined that the heart has its own complex nervous system and sends far more messages to the brain than the brain sends to the heart. His research also concluded that the heart signals especially affect the brain centers involved in decision making, creativity, and emotional experience.[4]

Accessing the unique "mini-brain" of your heart can help calm the nervous system of your entire body, thus creating the environment for you to come back to presence. This is how I know when I'm triggered, worrying, or thinking too hard; one of the most reliable ways I return to presence is to tune into my intelligence of my heart. Here are some simple strategies that will help you access the intelligence of your heart.

Feel Gratitude

If our Amygdala is triggered, we are essentially in survival mode. The orientation of our primal brain is to see what we don't have or what we're lacking. That was an important orientation when food and shelter were scarce. But now, in our modern world, our physical needs are for the most part met, but our primal brains don't always register the abundance. By intentionally focusing on the abundance of all that you have, you can transform how your brain is functioning.

The act of gratitude is very simple. It means to notice how much you *do* have instead of how much you don't have. Notice both the quality and quantity of the support you have around you, including loved ones, friends, and colleagues. Think about all the people and animals you love. Give thanks for the material items in your life such as your home, clothing, food, money, or job. Pay attention to how much you have the opportunity to impact others positively and how others impact you. You can even have gratitude for the things that feel like problems.

Many people keep gratitude journals, and it's been proven that people who write down things they are grateful before sleep tend to fall asleep and stay asleep longer. The practice of gratitude is proven to reduce blood pressure, improve stress-related illnesses, and alleviate symptoms of depression.

PRACTICE: Keeping a gratitude journal is great, but don't fret if you're not the journaling type. When I'm trying to go to sleep, I simply review my day in my head and notice how much I have to be grateful for that day. I think about things from simply being able to get out of bed and shower, to seeing my kids' faces, to serving my clients. I even have gratitude for the grocery bagger who helped me with my groceries. During the day when I have a few extra minutes while waiting for someone, instead of getting on my phone to check email or Facebook, I simply go into gratitude for what I've experienced that day and what is yet to come to fruition.

Engage in Something Creative

Engaging in something creative requires activating your frontal lobe, and it's nearly impossible to be both in your frontal lobe and Amygdala at the same time. The act of creation sets the stage for you to move away from your triggered state and into the higher functioning part of your brain. Engaging in something creative breeds more creativity so this is why I ask my clients to do something creative, particularly when they are feeling stuck or triggered.

Creativity is not restricted to those with artistic abilities or amazing talent; anyone can engage in something that's creative. Some of my favorite creative outlets are music, performing, looking at great art, cooking, or going to a stage show or concert. My clients engage in anything from playing in a band, jewelry making, choreography, costume design, woodworking, painting, sculpture, writing, filmmaking, and photography. It doesn't matter what you're doing, just as long as it's creative.

Steve Jobs said, "Creativity is just connecting things. When you ask creative people how they did something, they feel a little guilty because they didn't really do it, they just saw something. It seemed obvious to them after a while." I love this quote because when a person is in their creative energy, things tend to emerge rather effortlessly. For one client an idea seemingly came "out of the blue" that transformed their business when she was painting. Another client told me a story about how he got clarity on a major issue at work when he was working on his model airplane. Engaging in creativity requires both hemispheres of the brain to work together, so this is why when you're engaged in something creative, you may find solutions to other challenges you're facing. Creativity isn't just fun, but in many ways, it is one of the most productive things you can do as a leader.

PRACTICE: Even if you don't see yourself as a creative person, there is something you do that's creative. First, identify what that is. It could be cooking, the way you play with your kids, or how you dress. You don't have to go pick up another hobby (unless you're inspired to!), but I am inviting you to be present to the times you are creative. Bringing your attention to those times and really letting yourself be in the moment will open your heart and mind in ways that may surprise you!

Connect with Something Larger than Yourself

One of my favorite ways to open my heart is to connect with something larger than myself. Our Amygdala is so focused on survival and is inherently self-centered. When I'm feeling triggered, stressed, and tight, being able to connect with something larger than myself is profoundly helpful. When I say "connect" with something larger

I simply mean turn your attention to it. Be present with it. For example, when I'm outside I try to connect with nature. I notice the details of the trees, the ferns on the ground, and I listen to the birds. I intentionally pay attention to the fact that the natural world is so much bigger than I am, yet I notice I'm a part of it. Tuning into the size and enormity of it triggers a sense of feeling more expansive. From there, I often feel more gratitude and creativity.

Here are some things you could connect with that might help you feel more expansive:

- A body of water

- Huge trees

- Stars, moon, and/or space

- History: imagining the lives of those who have come before us

- God: any form that feels right for you

- The Universe

- Mountains

- Volunteering: helping a charity or reaching out to those in need

- Art: explore a gallery or museum

Again, the point of connecting with something larger than you is to get you out of your own head and to help stir your own expansiveness. Connecting to something outside of yourself is a sure-fire way to get you unstuck, and it almost always makes people feel more alive, connected, happy, and optimistic: all aspects of the power of heart energy.

Have Some Fun

This presence thing can sound like a lot of work, but it shouldn't be. In fact, sometimes the more we "try" to get out of our head or become present, the more resistant we become. It can become an internal tug of war where the only one losing is you. So when all else fails and you're feeling stuck, stressed, and cranky, lighten up and have some fun. Laugh, go play, do something that makes you happy. Happiness is one of the highest vibrations out there, and it comes right from the heart. Happiness, like most emotions, is contagious; so the great news about letting yourself have some fun and be happy is that you'll actually be helping those around you.

Think about the last few times you were really happy or at your best, and answer the below questions to help spark some ideas about how to get more of it in your life.

What activity brings you the most enjoyment or makes you happiest?

_____

_____

_____

_____

When's the last time you engaged in that activity?

_____

_____

_____

_____

What would it take for you to get more of that in your life? (i.e. asking for it, setting boundaries around your time for it, committing to it)

_____

_____

_____

_____

_____

_____

———————————————————————

———————————————————————

———————————————————————

———————————————————————

———————————————————————

———————————————————————

Even if you only get a bit more happiness and fun in your life, consider it a win. If you're completely at a loss for something that sounds fun, know that you're not a lost cause. This is unfortunately a hard reality of our overworked society, but we're not better for it. Leaders I work with are far more productive, creative, resourceful, and effective when they allow themselves to have some fun. Joy and happiness is our natural state, and if you're void of this from your life, it just means you've been working and living in a way that is so conditioned that you simply forgot about the importance of fun. If you've forgotten how to have fun, try one or more of these exercises to wake up your fun muscle.

- Write down all the things you loved to do as a child, then do one of those things.

- Call a friend that makes you laugh and ask to spend some time together.

- Go out for a guys' or gals' night.

- Watch a funny movie, even better if it was a movie that made you laugh when you were younger.

- Give yourself permission to do something decadent that you normally don't do.

- Set up a game night with friends or family.

- Watch funny YouTube videos.

- Attend a laughter workshop; that may sound contrived, but you'd be amazed at how effective it is!

Lightening up and having some fun isn't hard, but it can feel like work sometimes. The only "hard" part is getting out of your conditioned pattern to overwork. It's common to feel that you don't have time or that you may be above or beyond having fun, but these are just symptoms that you've lost connection with one of your most powerful (and productive!) parts of yourself—your heart and sense of joy. Every client I work with starts in this place, and they always thank me for pushing them to have more fun; not only do they feel better (and their spouses like them better), but they actually feel more effective at work, without working any harder.

GATEWAY #4: YOUR MIND

Spiritual teacher and author Eckhart Tolle is quoted as saying, "The mind is a superb instrument if used rightly. Used wrongly, however, it becomes very destructive." The concept of presence isn't about using the mind or freeing yourself from thought altogether, rather it's about being able to observe your mind and use its power intentionally.

Although much of this book is about how to get out of your head, we're now going to go over how you can use the power and focus of your mind to gain a deeper level of presence. The mind is designed to be in service to our wisdom and presence. It is the doorway we walk through to access that wisdom.

Unplug from Technology

Soren Gordhamer, author of *Wisdom 2.0: The New Movement Toward Purposeful Engagement in Business and Life,* states, "According to one study, a typical worker who sits at a computer checks his email more than fifty times a day and uses instant messaging seventy-seven times a day." He goes on to say, "It takes an average of 16 minutes and 33 seconds for a worker interrupted by an email to get back on track to what he or she was doing." As long as our minds are constantly fragmented and interrupted and as long as we're operating in such a fragmented way, we don't have access to either the power of our minds or our deeper wisdom.

In our overly connected world, the thought of unplugging from technology can be both anxiety producing and liberating. Technology "vacations" are becoming increasingly more popular too. That's when people announce via their numerous social media outlets that they are unplugging for a period of time. The company Digital Detox, based in San Francisco, offers retreats where all participants are required to check in their electronics for the duration of the retreat, usually a weekend. Our inability to unplug has become such an issue that people are literally paying thousands of dollars to disconnect, so they can reconnect to their inner world and to others in a more meaningful way.

I won't pretend that unplugging from technology is easy. Remember, the varied and intermittent stimulus gives us a hit of dopamine—one of the "feel good" chemicals in our brain. From our brain's perspective, that constant stimulus is not that different from being addicted to cocaine. So if you feel anxious at the thought of giving up your "drug," it makes sense. Your brain has become accustomed to getting a hit of dopamine. The great news is you can make a choice to pull away.

PRACTICE: I invite you to take a "technology vacation," and give your brain some time away from constant stimulation. You might be amazed with what happens when you have time without constant input. Like with any habit or addiction, you will go through a withdrawal period. Plan for it, and know what you're going to do instead of picking up your phone or checking email.

Use Anchor Words

Many people use meditation as a way to quiet the mind and tune in to inner wisdom. I have found even the word meditation brings up a lot of connotations for people, both positive and negative. I have experimented with formal meditation over the years, and in the beginning, I would get frustrated or antsy trying to meditate. Something that worked for me was using "anchor words," a concept I learned when I attended mindfulness training at the School for Mindfulness in California.

Anchor Words is a way to simply label what you're experiencing while you focus on breathing. It's not that you're trying to quiet the mind, but rather you are objectively observing it. For example, when I was practicing being mindful of my breath by sitting quietly and breathing in and out, I noticed that my back started to mildly twitch, and I said to myself "sensation." When my mind began to wander toward something I needed to do, I said to myself, "thought." When I began to feel anxious, I said to myself, "feeling." The idea is to simply observe your experience without judging it. That is the definition of mindfulness: to be present in the moment, on purpose, and without judgment. The experience of using Anchor Words helped me tune in at a deeper level, and every time I use this practice, my mind and body feel more connected and centered than ever before.

> **PRACTICE:** Try your own version of Anchor Words. You can use this anytime and anywhere. You can try to meditate, or you can use this when sitting in a waiting room or waiting in line. The point is using your mind to help tune in by deeply focusing it on what you're experiencing in the moment. Remember, it doesn't work if you judge your experience, just observe.

"Marinate" in What You Want

I recently had a conversation with a client who is the president of a mid-sized real-estate company in Seattle. She told me how stretched thin her staff was with the recent recovery of the real estate market, and how finding another highly specialized manager would really help. In the very next breath she explained how impossible it was going to be to find someone, because this person would need a certain level of training and experience, plus be able to work crazy hours and be great with the staff. For my client, this was the impossible dream.

I explained that when we want something, especially if it feels darn near impossible, the best way to go about it is to first go inward and "marinate" in what we want, while simultaneously taking the outward actions we know to take. Marinating means to imagine, daydream, or visualize in great detail about what it would feel like to have what you want. Marinating is often the missing ingredient in creating exactly what we want.

My client had created the job description, networked, and gotten the word out, and she got desperate enough to hire a headhunter. Nothing was working, and she admitted she was desperate. I asked her to give the situation two more weeks before she did anything too crazy (like hire a less qualified person), and I encouraged her to marinate in what she wanted. I asked her to think about what it would feel like knowing she had the new manager in place. I told her to feel the relief and joy knowing everyone would feel more supported being fully staffed with the right people. I asked her to think about how her staff would feel knowing they had a great manager in place. I even asked her to think about how good it would feel to the new manager knowing she was part of her great company. Marinating is using the power of your mind (and heart!) to create—behind your eyes first—what you want to create in front of your eyes later.

In less than two weeks a "perfect" candidate showed up at the office. She had just moved to Seattle from Phoenix and settled in to her new apartment. She focused on finding a job and was excited to find my client's posting. My client couldn't believe how "perfect" the fit was. In fact, she said it played out almost exactly the way she had imagined it. I have taken literally hundreds of clients through this process, and all of them get what they want or darn close!

PRACTICE: When you want to create something in your life or leadership, take the outward actions you know to take, but don't forget the importance of marinating or daydreaming about what it would feel like to actually have what you want. It might just make its way to you faster than you think possible!

(LEARN MORE)

BEING PRESENT, FIRST with yourself and then with others may be one of the greatest gifts we have access to. Being present is an act of compassion, respect, and dignity, and it's what every human is hungry for—to be heard, seen, and respected by another. The great news is that we have an opportunity to share this gift as often and as generously as we want. The act of presence doesn't take anything away from us, and in fact, it gives us energy because we're returning to our natural state. Your presence allows you to access an infinite supply of energy, wisdom, and compassion, and our world is in need of as much of that as we can get right now. Presence can not only change your life, but it can change the world. May your life and those you touch be forever changed for the better as a result of you strengthening your presence.

Get Present: Simple Strategies to Get Out of Your Head and Lead More Powerfully is a part of a larger, more in depth book called *Get Out of Your Head: How the Practice of Presence Can Transform Your Leadership and Life* due out Fall of 2014.

If you like what you've read in this book, I invite you to visit www.yaoconsulting.com. Sign up to receive my special report, "Five Ways to Dilute Your Impact as a Leader (and how to stop!)". When you sign up, you'll also get access to "The Whole Leader" podcast show in which I interview several thought leaders about presence and leadership.

These thought leaders include:

Maria Gonzalez, Author of *Mindful Leadership: 9 Ways to Self-Awareness, Transforming Yourself and Inspiring Others*

Chris Murchison, Vice President of Staff Development and Culture at Hopelab in San Francisco. Hopelab is an innovative research company focused on developing conscious leadership.

Marie-Rose Phan-Lê, Award Winning Film Director and Producer of the film *Talking Story*— an original documentary that explores the spiritual and healing traditions of indigenous cultures worldwide.

Molly Gordon, Owner of Shaboom Inc. and author of *The Way of the Accidental Entrepreneur,* helping leaders create mastery and meaning. Master Certified Coach in private practice since 1996.

⟨ NOTES ⟩

1. Gilbert, Jason. 2012, August 16, *Huffington Post,* http://www.huffingtonpost.com, "Smartphone Addiction: Staggering Percentage of Humans Couldn't Go One Day Without Their Phones." Original poll by *TIME Magazine,* Techland Section.

2. Poitras, Colin. *The Journal of Nutrition.* February 1, 2012 vol. 142 "Mild Dehydration Affects Mood in Healthy Young Women, " *UConn Today,* University of Connecticut

3. Jeffrey S. Durmer, M.D., Ph.D.and David F. Dinges, Ph.D.; "Neurocognitive Consequences of Sleep Deprivation," University of Pennsylvania, SEMINARS IN NEUROLOGY/VOLUME 25, NUMBER 1 2005 pages 117-129. http://www.med.upenn.edu/uep/user_documents/dfd3.pdf

4. Armour, J.A., M.D., Ph.D, "The Little Brain on the Heart" *Cleveland Clinic Journal of Medicine,* Volume 74, Supplement 1, February 2007. Armour, J.A., Center of Research, Sacred Heart Hospital, University of Montreal, Montreal, Quebec, Canada

(ACKNOWLEDGMENTS)

THERE HAVE BEEN MANY people who have helped me learn and expand along the way and I couldn't have written the content of this book without them. Thank you Marie-Rose Phan-Lê, Annie Duggan, and Michael for helping me come into my own presence in profound ways and for seeing me in ways I couldn't yet see.

The book literally could not have been written without Brooke Warner, writing coach extraordinaire, who simultaneously held my hand and kicked my behind for several months; nor could it have been written without Molly Gordon, who inspired my closeted creative to come out and play.

A big thank you to Mom and Dad for showing me what leadership looks like in all its various forms and for encouraging it in me from early on; and to my dear boys Ethan and Logan for teaching me so much about presence by accepting nothing less than my full attention.

Thank you to my loving husband, Jesse Yao, for supporting me, picking me up, cheering me on, and challenging me along every step of this crazy ride together. I truly wouldn't be where I am today without you.

Last, but not least, a big thank you to all of my clients who have taught me so much about presence, commitment, and leadership. Your contributions to the world continue to inspire me and I consider it an honor to stand beside you.

(ABOUT THE AUTHOR)

© Ingrid Pape-Sheldon

SARA HARVEY YAO is an executive coach who specializes in helping leaders strengthen their presence by gaining access to the wisdom of their head, heart, and gut. She has developed and trained more than 3,500 leaders in six countries. Sara's coaching skills are favored by countless executives from leading companies, among them

Microsoft, Coldwell Banker Bain, and Coinstar. Companies eagerly invest in Sara's expertise because she has an impeccable track record for helping leaders gain immense self-awareness, expand their influence, and create a more compelling presence. Whether working one-on-one, as a facilitator, presenting in front of large audiences, Sara is committed to guiding clients to clarity about behaviors, ego tactics, and influencing styles that hamper conscious leadership.

Sara is a mother of two boys, Ethan and Logan, and has been married to her husband Jesse since 1998. She's a constant seeker of truth and wisdom and is committed to leading by inspiration and living in the moment in every aspect of her full life.

CPSIA information can be obtained at www.ICGtesting.com
Printed in the USA
BVOW07s1820121213

338830BV00001B/1/P